CONTENTS

It's a White World   4

Stowe Mountain   6

Val d'Isère   8

Whistler   10

Sierra Nevada   12

Thredbo   14

Air & Style   16

Jackson Hole   18

Snow Park   20

Winter X Games   22

Verbier   24

Åre   26

Chamonix   28

Glossary   30

Finding Out More   31

Index   32

It's a White World

You push yourself to your feet and brush the snow from your bottom. The board starts to slide downhill. You let it pick up speed, then drop into a long, arcing turn. A fan of snow sprays up behind the board in the sunshine. Sound good? Only a snowboarder knows the feeling!

Dragging a hand as he carves a turn through the powdery snow, this rider is having a GREAT day.

SNOWBOARDING WORLD

At any moment in time, there is a snowboarding slope open somewhere in the world. But how can you be sure you'd fit in if you arrived there, ready to ride? You don't want people to think you're a **kook**. So you'll need to know the rules of the game: how to keep yourself and other people safe in the dangerous mountain environment. You need to understand snowboarding's secret language – what's a "heel-edge to toe-edge turn"? And most important of all, you need to know how to snowboard.

THE SECRET LANGUAGE OF SNOWBOARDING

kook clumsy, untidy rider
piste marked route for
   skiers and snowboarders

"Let's go that way." "No, over there!" Nothing beats the excitement of hitting the slope with your friends.

PASSPORT TO SNOWBOARDING

Almost everything you need to know about snowboarding is gathered together in this book. It's your passport to the snowboarding world! Equipment, technique and other essentials are included. Now imagine you have a dream ticket that takes you anywhere in the world. Where would you go? Turn the page to start finding out!

Technical: Snowboarding equipment

There are a few basic bits of snowboarding gear everyone needs: a board, boots, and warm clothes. Most of these can be hired for a first trip. Once they've got the bug, riders often buy their own kit.

Clothing essentials:

• A waterproof jacket, ideally with a snow skirt (an inner layer with a hem that grips the hips tightly, to stop snow getting inside when you fall over).

• Waterproof trousers.

• Fleece, hat, goggles, snowboard gloves, thermal underwear, warm socks.

Board choices:

• Freestyle boards are symmetrical (the same shape front and back) and are good for jumps and riding in snow parks.

• Freeride boards have slightly longer noses and are good for **piste** and all-mountain riding.

Boots and bindings:

• Most riders use soft boots and strap bindings, which you have to sit down to fasten or unfasten.

• Some riders prefer step-in bindings, which automatically attach the boot to the board (so there's less sitting in the snow!).

Stowe Mountain

There are lots of resorts in this area of north-eastern America, so why pick Stowe? Simple: the nearby town of Burlington is home to the company that invented the modern snowboard, Burton. If you had to pick a place where they know their snowboard equipment, this is it! It also helps that Stowe has some great riding for boarders of all abilities.

STOWE MOUNTAIN
Location: Vermont, USA
Type of riding: piste, some powder areas
Difficulty level: 1 of 5
Season: November to April

SNOWBOARDING STOWE

This is a friendly resort, and the locals aren't snooty towards outsiders. The riding at Stowe includes Mount Mansfield, the highest peak in Vermont. Mansfield is best for experienced riders. Beginners tend to head for a separate area, Spruce Peak, where the runs are less steep and easier.

Snowboarding on a beautiful sunny day, on the slopes near Stowe.

THE SECRET LANGUAGE OF SNOWBOARDING

powder light, fluffy snow

If you like Stowe Mountain...

... you could also try:
- Jackson Hole, USA
- Chamonix, France
- Zermatt, Switzerland

EQUIPMENT

Snowboard: A freeride board is probably best for Stowe, which has 35 kilometres (21.7 miles) of pistes and fast, modern lifts. Expert boarders will want to try the **powder** at the Tres Amigos and Lookout areas.

Clothing: Wrap up warm for the chilly New England winds! A jacket with a hood to keep out the cold, and plenty of layers, are a good idea.

Other kit: Goggles, backpack for keeping spare clothes in.

Tip from a Local

Take a packed lunch – the mountain restaurants are always jam-packed!

SKILL
Hiring a board and kit

There's nothing worse than getting to the top of a mountain and discovering a problem with your hired equipment. These tips will help you make sure you get the right board, boots and bindings from a rental shop, wherever you are:

- Get the right length board: for most beginners, this is a board that comes up to their chin.
- Make sure your boots fit: you need a bit of wriggle room for your toes when your heel is right at the back of the boot. Make sure the boots are well padded, and that the tops don't bite into your calves.
- Check that the bindings fit the boots properly and are not too big. Double-check that all the nuts and bolts on the bindings are done up tightly.

Wearing boots that fit well and are comfortable makes snowboarding a much more enjoyable experience. It's worth spending time in the hire shop to get the right fit.

Val d'Isère

If you like company, Val d'Isère is the place for you. This is one of the busiest, loudest, liveliest resorts in the French Alps. From here you can get access to over 300 kilometres (186 miles) of runs, plus a huge variety of **off-piste** skiing. With all those runs, there are plenty of lifts for beginners to practise getting on and off.

SNOWBOARDING VAL D'ISÈRE

Val d'Isère and the nearby resort of Tignes (a good place to head for if you get tired of the crowds) make up the area called the Espace Killy. Almost half the runs (24 out of 55) are good for beginners. There is also a snow park and a **half pipe** for practising jumps.

VAL D'ISÈRE
Location: Savoie region, France
Type of riding: piste, some powder areas
Difficulty level: 1 of 5
Season: November to May

one of the biggest, busiest resorts in the Alps, Val d'Isère gives access to a huge snowboarding area.

Tip from a Local
Don't leave your last run of the day too late – the routes back into town get unbelievably crowded.

EQUIPMENT

Snowboard: Any kind of board is fine here. With all the lifts (24 of them tricky **drag lifts**) this might be a good place for step-in bindings.

Clothing: Like everywhere in the Alps, the weather can change quickly. Check the weather forecast (called *Metéo*) at the lift stations, but always take an extra layer of clothes just in case.

Other kit: Goggles, and your biggest, coolest sunglasses – the cafés and restaurants are a bit of a fashion parade!

THE SECRET LANGUAGE OF SNOWBOARDING

off-piste away from the marked, prepared ski areas

half pipe deep semi-circular channel cut into the snow

drag lift lift using a disc on the end of a telescopic pole to drag you uphill

SKILL
catching a lift

The lifts in mountain resorts were designed for skiers, not snowboarders – which can make them a bit of a challenge to use. The most common type of lift is a chair lift. Here's how to get on one:

Resting your board on the footrest, like the rider on the right, makes riding a chair lift with a snowboard much more comfortable.

1. In the lift queue, take your back foot out of the binding.

2. When the lift gate opens, slide or shuffle forwards, by pushing off with your back foot like a skateboarder.

3. Stop on the line. When the lift hits the back of your leg, sit down.

4. Pull the safety bar down (if it doesn't come down automatically) and rest your front leg on the footrest.

Whistler

Whistler bills itself as the world's best snowboard destination, and there are plenty of boarders who agree. If the winter days just aren't long enough for you, the resort offers night-time riding, and even summer boarding. There are also three snow parks and three half pipes.

WHISTLER
Location: British Columbia, Canada
Type of riding: piste, powder, snow parks
Difficulty level: 2 of 5
Season: November to June

SNOWBOARDING WHISTLER

There really is something for everyone at Whistler. Most of the pistes are best for intermediate riders, but there are still 40 that are great for beginners. As most people learning to snowboard stick to the same three or four pistes, that means there are plenty to choose from. Expert thrill seekers, meanwhile, can drop off cliffs, ride through powder fields, or launch massive **airs** in the snow park.

Getting a friend to hold on to you for your first go might seem like a good idea – but really it's best to get used to balancing on your own.

SKILL
Balancing on the board

You've got your board, and you've managed to catch a lift to a nice-looking slope to start on. It's time to take the first steps to becoming an expert snowboarder:

1. Sit in the snow and strap on your board (do up your leash first, in case the board slides away).

2. Push yourself to your feet, digging your heels into the snow for grip.

3. Once you are used to balancing, put a little extra weight on your front foot.

The board will slide in that direction.

4. To stop, take the extra weight off your front foot. Now put weight on your back foot, and the board will slide in the opposite direction. That's it – you're snowboarding.

At Whistler, beginners can practise their wobbly first moves in areas called Slow Zones. High speeds are not allowed here, which makes it a more relaxing (and safer) place to learn.

EQUIPMENT

Snowboard: Bring whatever kind of board is most suitable for the riding you plan to do.

Clothing: Lots of the pistes go through trees, so there is usually shelter. Even so, it gets cold, so wrap up well.

Other kit: A hooded jacket or balaclava might come in handy for keeping your ears warm on really freezing days.

Hooo-whee! Extreme riding at Whistler: fortunately, there are also slopes for less-expert riders.

THE SECRET LANGUAGE OF SNOWBOARDING

air or **"aerial"** this means a jump

Sierra Nevada

There can't be many places where you can ski with a view of Morocco's Rif Mountains. In fact, there's only ONE place where you can do that: Sierra Nevada in Spain. Closer to the resort are the amazing ancient palaces of the Alhambra, and just a couple of hours away are the sunny beaches of the Mediterranean Sea.

SIERRA NEVADA
Location: Andalusia, Spain
Type of riding: mainly piste, some freestyle
Difficulty level: 1.5 of 5
Season: December to May

SNOWBOARDING SIERRA NEVADA

Despite being Europe's sunniest resort, Sierra Nevada has one of the longest ski seasons in Europe. If snow doesn't fall from the sky, they make it using snowmaking machines. The long, wide, rolling pistes are perfect for beginners and improvers to practise their techniques. Only expert snowboarders will struggle to find runs hard enough to challenge them.

Tip from a Local

At weekends and in high season, don't have a lie-in – by mid-morning, the lift queues are terrible!

The main run down into the resort at Sierra Nevada.

Sierra Nevada offers deep powder, as well as groomed pistes.

Heel-edge to toe-edge turns

This is the first proper turn most snowboarders make. Most riders sit down to do their bindings up, and then push up on to their heel edge before setting off down the slope.

1. Ride along on your heel edge, knees bent and weight on your front foot.

2. Let your knees drop forwards, putting pressure through your toes and shins. Your hands and shoulders also drop forwards and down.

3. As the board speeds up through the turn, keep the same body position. If you chicken out, it will race off downhill or **spin out**, and you'll crash.

4. Once the board has turned all the way round, on to the toe edge, relax into your original body position.

This rider has a nice, relaxed stance as she comes out of a heel-edge to toe-edge turn.

EQUIPMENT

Snowboard: A freeride board is probably best here, as most of the snowboarding is on-piste.

Clothing: High winds are common in winter (and sometimes close the lifts), so a windproof jacket and trousers. Light clothing is OK at the end of the season.

Other kit: Don't forget your suntan lotion!

THE SECRET LANGUAGE OF SNOWBOARDING

spin out let the board slip out of control

Thredbo

Say "Australia" and most people think of surfing, not snowboarding. But there IS snowboarding in Australia, and some of the country's best runs are found at Thredbo. The resort has the highest **vertical drop** in Australia, so the pistes are among the longest you can find.

THREDBO
Location: New South Wales, Australia
Type of riding: mainly piste, some off-piste and freestyle
Difficulty level: 2 of 5
Season: June to October

SNOWBOARDING THREDBO

At Thredbo, two-thirds of the pistes are ideal for improvers. The resort can suffer from lack of snow, but it has good snowmaking machines and most runs can be ridden right through the season. When it DOES snow, expert riders head for the Central Spur area, where the powder can be great.

Picking a route through the rocks in one of Thredbo's off-piste areas.

Tip from a Local

In summer, the Supertrail (the resort's longest run) turns into the Thredbo Downhill, a killer mountain bike route.

EQUIPMENT

Snowboard: A freeride board is probably best here, but there is a good snow park if you want to practise your freestyle moves.

Clothing: It's usually below freezing at the top of the mountain in midwinter, so wrap up warm.

Other kit: Swimming goggles and costume: Thredbo has an Olympic-sized swimming pool.

SKILL
Toe-edge to heel-edge turns

Pick a wide, gentle slope for practising this turn. Until you are used to turning in a direction that's hard to see, it is best not to go too fast.

Midway through a long, drawn-out turn, on a beautifully groomed piste.

1. Ride along on your toe edge, knees bent and weight on your front foot.

2. Let your weight drop backwards into your bottom, putting pressure through your heels and into the tops of your feet. Lift your hands up and back towards your shoulders.

3. As the board speeds up through the turn, keep the same body position. It will help to look sideways, in the direction of the turn.

4. Once the board has turned all the way round, on to the heel edge, return to your original body position.

THE SECRET LANGUAGE OF SNOWBOARDING

vertical drop distance from top of highest run to bottom of lowest.

Air & Style

Each year, the Air & Style draws huge crowds to watch the snowboarding contests and live bands. Past winners include snowboarding legends such as Ingmar Backman, Terje Håkonsen, Jim Rippey and Shaun White. Today, this is one competition that every top snowboarder dreams of winning – the prize money is over US$250 000!

AIR & STYLE
Location: Innsbrück, Austria
Type of riding: big air, quarter pipe
Difficulty level: 5 of 5
Date: December each year

CONTEST ORIGINS

Air & Style started in 1993, when two friends decided to organize a contest to see who could do the best single jump. They expected a few hundred people to show up to watch, and were amazed when several thousand snowboard fans appeared at the gates. From there, Air & Style became one of the biggest snowboard contests anywhere.

Olivier Gittler stands ready to launch himself down the scary-looking start ramp at the Innsbrück Air & Style.

Tragedy in 1999

Tragedy struck the contest in 1999. When 45 000 spectators all tried to leave at once, six people died in the crush. The next year the contest moved to nearby Seefeld, and in 2005–07 it was held in Munich, Germany. From 2008, Air & Style returned to Innsbrück. (Another Air & Style is also held in Munich.)

Snowboard events

Air & Style uses two basic types of contest, **quarter pipe** and **big air**. Both are based around the idea of doing the biggest, trickiest jump possible. A panel of three judges decides the scores. Each rider gets three attempts, and their best score is the one that counts.

Twenty-four of the world's top snowboarders are invited to take part in the contest. There are two 12-rider knock-out rounds, then an eight-rider final.

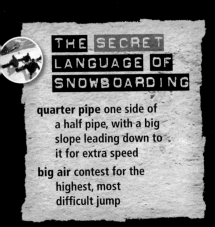

THE SECRET LANGUAGE OF SNOWBOARDING

quarter pipe one side of a half pipe, with a big slope leading down to it for extra speed

big air contest for the highest, most difficult jump

Finland's Eero Ettala midway through a massive, crowd-pleasing air.

Jackson Hole

Jackson Hole is one of the world's best resorts for riding steep, powder-snow slopes. It's not really a beginner's resort: only one of the 56 runs is earmarked for beginners. But if you know the basics and want to improve your off-piste riding, there is probably nowhere better to do it than here.

SNOWBOARDING JACKSON HOLE

Jackson Hole has the biggest vertical drop in the USA: the highest lift takes you over 3 kilometres (almost 2 miles) above sea level. The resort is good for improvers, and excellent for experts. Unusually for North America, there are few limits on off-piste snowboarding. The only downside is that when the weather is bad, it's SO bad it becomes impossible to snowboard.

JACKSON HOLE
Location: Wyoming, USA
Type of riding: most famous for steep runs and access to off-piste
Difficulty level: 3 of 5
Season: November to April

Getting a lift on a helicopter is one way to make sure your tracks are the first ones through Jackson Hole's back-country snow.

EQUIPMENT

Snowboard: There are two snow parks and a half pipe, so freestyle boards are OK. But people really come to Jackson for the powder: bring a freeride board.

Clothing: Pack your warmest clothes. Then pack some more warm clothes, hats, scarves, thermals, etc. It gets REALLY cold here.

Other kit: A balaclava and heated gloves (did we mention how cold it gets?).

THE SECRET LANGUAGE OF SNOWBOARDING

couloir narrow, steep-sided valley on a mountainside

SKILL
Riding in powder snow

The best place to practise riding powder snow is on a piste just after heavy snowfall.

Keep the nose up (the board's, not yours!), if you want to pull off turns like this one.

• For powder conditions, some riders move the bindings on their board back slightly, a little more towards the tail.

• In powder you will need to point more downhill than usual to get the board going.

• Keep your knees bent and your weight centred at first. When making turns, put more weight into your back foot than usual. (If you put weight on your front foot, the nose of the board will bury itself in the snow.)

• To turn, shift your body weight in the usual way. When making tight turns, some riders "bounce". They straighten their legs halfway through the turn, then go back into a bent-knees position.

19

Snow Park

At first glance, Snow Park appears a surprising choice as one of the great places to go snowboarding. It has no pistes, and just one lift – compared to the 200 pistes and 33 lifts at Whistler, Snow Park doesn't seem to have much to offer. Don't be fooled, though: this is one of the world's best places for practising your freestyle skills.

SNOW PARK
Location: Otago, South Island, New Zealand
Type of riding: freestyle
Difficulty level: 2.5 of 5
Season: June to October

SNOWBOARDING SNOW PARK

This is freestyle central. Snow Park (no prizes for guessing how they thought of the name…) is famous around the world as one of the best snow parks anywhere. It has obstacles and jumps to suit any snowboarder, from someone trying freestyle for the first time to experts practising their **stalefish grabs**.

Stylish (and very tricky) grabs like this one are a common sight at Snow Park.

THE SECRET LANGUAGE OF SNOWBOARDING

stalefish grab air in which the rider grabs the heel edge of the board behind the back leg, with his or her trailing hand.
ramp steep slope
lip edge of a half pipe

20

Jumps

Starting small, like this rider, and then building up to bigger jumps is the best way to increase your confidence.

Jumps are best learned once you're able to ride with the board flat on the snow, without either edge biting in.

1. Head for the **ramp** (pick a small one to start!) at moderate speed. Too fast will be out of control, but too slow will make for a heavy landing.

2. Slide up the ramp with the board flat on the snow. Bend your knees and hips as the board rises up the ramp.

3. As the board leaves the **lip** of the ramp, straighten your legs and hips to help it into the air.

4. As it drops back towards the snow, bend your knees to absorb the landing. Land slightly tail first, and with the board flat (rather than tilted towards either edge). Ride off with a big grin.

EQUIPMENT

Snowboard: Freestyle board, soft boots and strap bindings.

Clothing: No need to go overboard on cold-weather gear, and on a hot day it would be possible to wear just a T-shirt and snowboard pants.

Other kit: A helmet is definitely required.

Tip from a Local
Stay late for the floodlit night-riding sessions, and you're likely to spot top pro snowboarders trying out some new moves.

If you like Snow Park...
... you could also try:
• Whistler, Canada
• Niseko, Japan
The freestyle facilities at both are excellent.

Winter X Games

Since 2002, the Winter X Games have been held in Aspen, Colorado. The Games are a competition for extreme sports. The summer version features sports such as skateboarding, BMX and motocross. In winter, snowboarders, skiers and snowmobilers flock to Aspen for one of the biggest contests of the year.

Hot action in the half pipe at the 2009 Winter X Games.

SNOWBOARD EVENTS

The biggest draw is often the **slope style** contest. Riders take turns to put down the most difficult, most stylish sequence of airs possible. They use a variety of ramps to get the biggest possible height and **hang time** on each jump.

Shaun White – a.k.a. the Flying Tomato – hits it at the X Games. White is the only person to win at both Summer and Winter X Games. The summer one was for skateboarding.

The half-pipe contest also draws lots of fans. The finals often take place at night: the floodlights and big crowds make for an unforgettable atmosphere.

THE SECRET LANGUAGE OF SNOWBOARDING

slope style short freestyle course with a choice of jumps

hang time length of time spent in the air during a jump

THE FLYING TOMATO

The most successful X Games snowboarder of all time is sometimes called The Flying Tomato, because of his bushy red hair. His real name is Shaun White. Around the world,

White is known as one of the greats. He won the pipe contests at the X Games in 2003, 2006, 2008 and 2009, and the slope style in 2003–2006 and 2009. He also won half-pipe gold at the 2006 and 2010 Winter Olympics.

Verbier

Verbier has always been popular with the rich and famous. This is the kind of resort where you could find yourself sharing a lift with a movie star, a famous millionaire, or a member of a European royal family. But Verbier's steep slopes, good snow and off-piste runs also pull in hardened snowboarders from around the world.

VERBIER
Location: Valais, Switzerland
Type of riding: all kinds
Difficulty level: 3 of 5
Season: December to April

SNOWBOARDING VERBIER

Verbier has something for every kind of rider, whether beginner, improver or expert. There are three main areas: Verbier/Mont Fort, Savoleyres, and Bruson. Savoleyres is less steep than the other areas, so it's good for beginners and improvers. All three have good off-piste runs, and the snowboarding through the trees is among the best in Europe.

EQUIPMENT

Snowboard: Whatever kind of board you want to bring, Verbier has runs that will suit it. For **boardercross**, a freestyle board is best.

Clothing: As always in the mountains, it pays to be prepared for cold weather even on a warm day. For boardercross you will need a helmet.

Other kit: An **avalanche transceiver** if you go off-piste, and your best designer sunglasses – this is one of Europe's most fashionable resorts.

THE SECRET LANGUAGE OF SNOWBOARDING

- **boardercross** race down an obstacle course of gates, banked turns and jumps
- **avalanche transceiver** electonic device that sends a signal to locate people buried in an avalanche
- **hole shot** first place at the first bend

Tip from a Local

Ask the ski patrollers in the Freeride huts where to find the best snow conditions that day.

22

SKILL
The hole shot

Verbier has two boardercross courses, which both hold exciting races regularly through the season. Like most boardercross areas, they are open to ordinary riders whenever there is no racing going on.

1. At the start, the riders line up side by side.

2. When the start signal goes, they launch themselves down the slope. Getting the **hole shot** makes it much more likely you will win, mainly

If you like to watch snowboarders crashing, head to a boardercross competition! You won't have to wait long for one to happen.

because it makes it LESS likely that someone will crash into you.

3. The tight bends and big jumps of the course mean there are plenty of spectacular crashes. Often, the winner crosses the line first simply by not crashing.

If you like Verbier...

… you could also try:
- Aspen, USA
- Gstaad, Switzerland
- St Anton, Austria

Each is great for star-spotting.

A rider competes in Xtreme Verbier, part of the Freeride World Tour.

Åre

ÅRE
Location: Jamtland, Sweden
Type of riding: piste runs, some off-piste, but famous for freestyle
Difficulty level: 3.5 of 5
Season: November to May

Åre (pronounced "oo-ah-ray") offers a different kind of snowboarding experience from almost anywhere else. At the end of the season it is possible to ride for almost 24 hours, as the sun hardly sets. In midwinter the sun hardly rises, and the resort's floodlights fire up to light the way through the dark for snowboarders.

Practising a rail slide at one of Åre's freestyle parks.

SNOWBOARDING ÅRE

Only five of Åre's 98 pistes are designed for experts, so the resort's runs are best for beginners and improvers. There are lots of drag lifts, which gets tiresome after a while. BUT expert snowboarders still come here – why? The answer lies in the three snow parks and, especially, Åre's half pipe.

Tip from a Local
If the slopes are busy, go home, have a nap, and then go riding at night – it's much less crowded.

SKILL

Riding half pipe

Riding the half pipe well is one of snowboarding's biggest challenges. The steep slopes and high jumps make this a dangerous activity. Snowboarders have developed a few rules to make it as safe as possible:

• Wait your turn at the top of the pipe. Don't try and **drop in** halfway down.

• Only drop in when the rider ahead of you has finished his or her run.

• If you fall, your turn is over – ride straight out of the pipe. Don't try to climb back up the sides or to gain speed again.

• Keep a friendly face: cheer others and encourage them, even if they're not very good. Everyone was a beginner once.

If you like Åre...

... you could also try:
• Méribel, France

EQUIPMENT

Snowboard: A freestyle board and soft boots would be best. There are some good piste runs, but for snowboarders this resort is mainly about the snow parks and half pipe.

Clothing: Depends on the time of year. In winter, it can be extremely cold and you'll need all your warmest gear. At the end of the season, you might see people riding in shorts.

THE SECRET LANGUAGE OF SNOWBOARDING

drop in start riding a slope or ramp

Warming up for a contest run in the half pipe. The sprayed-on blue lines help the riders spot the lip of the pipe, so they know exactly where they need to land.

27

Chamonix

Say the name "Chamonix" to an expert snowboarder and his or her eyes will light up. The steepness, challenging slopes and breathtaking beauty of this valley in the French Alps are famous the world over. Chamonix has been a magnet for mountain-lovers for over 100 years.

CHAMONIX
Location: Haute Savoie, France
Type of riding: good piste runs, but famous for off-piste
Difficulty level: 4 of 5
Season: December to April

Chamonix has all kinds of boarding, but really it's famous for just one thing: extreme, experts-only riding

If you like Chamonix...

... go to Chamonix. There really isn't anywhere else like it.

SNOWBOARDING CHAMONIX

There are five or six snowboarding areas spread up and down the Chamonix Valley, some of which have to be reached by bus from the town centre. Over everything towers Mont Blanc, Europe's highest mountain. Expert boarders come here for the long, steep off-piste riding, but there are also some good piste runs. There is a great snow park in the Grands Montets ski area.

EQUIPMENT

Snowboard: Bring a freeride board that you are 100 per cent comfortable riding. This is NOT a place to be trying out new gear.

Clothing: The best possible clothing for warmth and windproofness. Some of the snowboarding is high up and it can take a long time to get down if the weather changes.

Other kit: Backpack for gear; avalanche transceiver if you plan on going off-piste; emergency blankets for warmth; mobile phone.

Tip from a Local

If there's fresh powder, get up ready to catch the first lift of the day (which you'll be sharing with some of the world's best freeriders).

SKILL
Riding off-piste

Off-piste snowboarding is thrilling, but it is also extremely dangerous. The safest way to go off-piste is with a local guide, who will adapt your route to suit your skill level.

It might be hard work getting to the top – but it will all become worthwhile on the way down.

• A full off-piste kit includes: climbing harness, an ice axe, crampons, snowshoes, a transceiver, a snow probe, a shovel, a 40-metre (131-foot) rope, an ice screw, two slings, two ascenders, four screw-gate karabiners – and a BIG backpack for carrying it all.

• You are responsible for your own actions and safety. If you are uncomfortable with anything, retreat.

• Never try anything you feel you cannot safely achieve – it could be fatal.

• Look up, down, and all around: is there anything further up the slope, down the slope, or to the sides that could be dangerous?

• Dangers include layers of snow that could cause an avalanche, hidden cliffs and rocks.

Glossary

Words from the Secret Language features

air or **"aerial"** this means a jump

avalanche transceiver electronic device that sends a signal to locate people buried in an avalanche

big air contest for the highest, most difficult jump

boardercross race down an obstacle course of gates, banked turns and jumps

couloir narrow, steep-sided valley on a mountainside

drag lift lift using a disc on the end of a telescopic pole to drag you uphill

drop in start riding a slope or ramp

half pipe deep semi-circular channel cut into the snow

hang time length of time spent in the air during a jump

hole shot first place at the first bend

kook clumsy, untidy rider

lip edge of a half pipe

off-piste away from the marked, prepared ski areas

piste marked route for skiers and snowboarders

powder light, fluffy snow

quarter pipe one side of a half pipe, with a big slope leading down to it for extra speed

ramp steep slope

slope style short freestyle course with a choice of jumps

spin out let the board slip out of control

stalefish grab air in which the rider grabs the heel edge of the board behind the back leg, with his or her trailing hand

vertical drop distance from top of highest run to bottom of lowest

Other words riders use

angles refers to the angles at which a rider's bindings are set. Most riders have their front binding between 10 and 20 degrees forwards, and their back binding between 3 degrees forwards and 3 degrees backwards.

binding plate and straps that allow the boots to be attached to the snowboard

board snowboard

boot snowboard boot

bubble small closed lift for 4 to 6 people

cable car (also sometimes called a gondola) large, closed-in lift that several people can stand in at once

chair lift lift on which between 4 and 10 people can sit

deck either the top of the snowboard or, sometimes, the whole board

edge metal strip on the bottom edge of the board

freeride snowboarding on or off piste, but on natural landscape

freestyle snowboarding in a snow park, half pipe or some other artificial landscape

nose front quarter of the snowboard

riding snowboarding

tail back quarter of the snowboard

Finding Out More

THE INTERNET

www.skiclub.co.uk/skiclub/default.aspx
The home site of the Ski Club of Great Britain is a wonderful resource for skiers and snowboarders everywhere. It gives details of hundreds of resorts, up-to-date information on snowfall, advice on safety, health and fitness, and much more.

www.worldsnowboardguide.com
This site does a similar job to the Ski Club one, but is aimed more directly at snowboarders. Combining information from the two sites gives a very clear idea of what a resort is like. The added bonus of the World Snowboard site is that it gives an ever-changing top 10 best resorts in each country.

www.goneboarding.co.uk
Big English-language online snowboarding community site, with forums, news, reviews, classified ads – all the things you'd hope to find.

BOOKS

Footprint travel guides do a good series of books for adventure-sports fans, including:

Snowboarding the World Matt Barr, Chris Moran and Ewan Wallace (Footprint, 2006)

Skiing Europe Matt Barr and Gabriella le Breton (Footprint, 2008)

MAGAZINES

Whitelines
One of the oldest and best snowboard magazines in the UK, with great features, interviews, trick tips and advice for snowboarders of all ability levels. The magazine has a good website too at **www.whitelines.com**.

Snowboard
US-produced magazine carries similar information to *Whitelines*, but from a North American viewpoint. Has a good website, at **www.snowboard-mag.com**, with a useful Buyer's Guide section telling you all about the best gear.

Index

air (aerial) 10, 11, 17, 23
Air & Style 16–17
Alps, France 8, 28
Åre, Sweden 26–27
Aspen, USA 22, 25
avalanche transceiver 24, 29
avalanches 24, 29

Backman, Ingmar 16
backpack 7, 29
balancing 10
big air 17
bindings 5, 7, 9, 13, 19
boardercross 24, 25
boards 5, 7
    freeride 5, 7, 13, 15, 19, 29
    freestyle 5, 19, 21, 24, 27
boots 5, 7, 21, 27

Chamonix, France 7, 28–29
clothing 5, 7, 9, 11, 13, 15, 19,
    21, 24, 27, 29

dropping in 27

equipment 5, 7, 9, 11, 13, 15,
    19, 21, 24, 27, 29
    hiring 7
Espace Killy, France 8
Ettala, Eero 17

Gittler, Olivier 16
gloves 5, 19
goggles 5, 7, 9
Gstaad, Switzerland 25

Håkonsen, Terje 16
half pipe 8, 9, 10, 17, 20, 22,
    23, 26, 27
hang time 23
heel-edge to toe-edge turns
    4, 13
helicopter 19
helmet 21, 24
hole shot 24, 25

Innsbrück, Austria 16–17

Jackson Hole, USA 7, 18–19
jumps 5, 8, 11, 16, 17, 20, 21,
    23, 24, 25, 27

leash 10
lifts 8, 9, 13, 18, 20, 26

Méribel, France 27
Mont Blanc, France 29
Mount Mansfield, USA 6
Munich, Germany 23

Niseko, Japan 21

off-piste 8, 9, 14, 18, 24, 26,
    28, 29

pistes/piste runs 4, 5, 6, 7, 8,
    10, 11, 12, 14, 15, 19, 20,
    24, 26, 27, 28
powder snow 4, 6, 7, 8, 10, 12,
    14, 18, 19, 29

quarter pipe 17

ramps 20, 21
Rif Mountains, Morocco 12
Rippey, Jim 16

St Anton, Austria 25
Sierra Nevada, Spain 12–13
slope style 23
Snow Park, New Zealand
    20–21
snow parks 5, 10, 15, 19, 20,
    26, 27, 29
snow skirt 5
snowmaking machines 12, 14
spinning out 13
Spruce Peak, USA 6
stalefish grab 20
Stowe Mountain, USA 6–7

Thredbo, Australia 14–15
Tignes, France 8
toe-edge to heel-edge turns 15
turns 4, 13, 15, 19

Val d'Isère, France 8–9
Verbier, Switzerland 24–25

weather forecast 9
Whistler, Canada 10–11, 21
White, Shaun 16, 23
Winter Olympics 23
Winter X Games 22–23

Xtreme Verbier 25

Zermatt, Switzerland 7